IN THE ZONE

TENNIS

DON WELLS

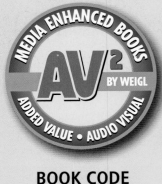

MEDIA ENHANCED BOOKS
AV² BY WEIGL
ADDED VALUE • AUDIO VISUAL

BOOK CODE

J680928

AV² by Weigl brings you media enhanced books that support active learning.

AV² provides enriched content that supplements and complements this book. Weigl's AV² books strive to create inspired learning and engage young minds for a total learning experience.

Go to **www.av2books.com**, and enter this book's unique code. You will have access to video, audio, web links, quizzes, a slide show, and activities.

Audio
Listen to sections of the book read aloud.

Video
Watch informative video clips.

Web Link
Find research sites and play interactive games.

Try This!
Complete activities and hands-on experiments.

Due to the dynamic nature of the Internet, some of the URLs and activities provided as part of AV² by Weigl may have changed or ceased to exist. AV² by Weigl accepts no responsibility for any such changes. All media enhanced books are regularly monitored to update addresses and sites in a timely manner. Contact AV² by Weigl at 1-866-649-3445 or av2books@weigl.com with any questions, comments, or feedback.

Published by AV² by Weigl
350 5th Avenue, 59th Floor
New York, NY 10118
Website: www.av2books.com   www.weigl.com

Library of Congress Cataloging-in-Publication Data

Wells, Donald.
 Tennis : in the zone / Don Wells.
   p. cm.
 Includes index.
 ISBN 978-1-60596-904-6 (alk. paper) -- ISBN 978-1-60596-905-3 (alk. paper) -- ISBN 978-1-60596-906-0
 1. Tennis--Juvenile literature. I. Title.
 GV996.5.W454 2011
 796.342--dc22

                              2009050264

Printed in the United States in North Mankato, Minnesota
1 2 3 4 5 6 7 8 9 14 13 12 11 10

052010
WEP264000

PROJECT COORDINATOR Heather C. Hudak   **DESIGN** Terry Paulhus

Every reasonable effort has been made to trace ownership and to obtain permission to reprint copyright material. The publishers would be pleased to have any errors or omissions brought to their attention so that they may be corrected in subsequent printings.

Weigl acknowledges Getty Images as its primary image supplier for this title.

CONTENTS

4 What is Tennis?

6 Getting Ready to Play

8 The Tennis Court

10 Keeping Score

12 Rules of the Court

14 Playing the Game

16 Superstars of the Sport

18 Superstars of Today

20 Staying Healthy

22 Tennis Brain Teasers

23 Glossary / Index

24 Log on to www.av2books.com

What is Tennis?

Tennis requires a great deal of strength and skill.

The game of tennis played today developed from lawn tennis. Major Walter C. Wingfield of England created the game in 1873. The first lawn tennis game was played between two players at a garden party in Wales. It was played on an hourglass-shaped grass court. The court was 30 yards (27 meters) wide at the **baselines** and 21 yards (19 m) wide at the net. Wingfield also published the first lawn tennis rulebook.

■ Tennis became a popular sport for women in the early 1900s.

In 1877, the All-England Croquet Club held the first Wimbledon Lawn Tennis Championships. Three club members wrote a set of rules for the **tournament**. The rules from this tournament are still used today.

Today, tennis is rarely played on grass. Tennis courts are usually made of concrete, asphalt, or clay. Tennis games can be played indoors or outdoors. Two to four players use rackets to hit a ball back and forth over a net that divides the court. Tennis played between two players is called "singles." Tennis with four players is called "doubles."

Tennis is one of the most popular **spectator** and participation sports in the world. It has fans and **competitors** in more than 100 countries.

Tennis does not require much equipment. A tennis ball is hollow and made of **inflated** rubber covered with fabric. The fabric may be wool or **synthetic**. Most tennis balls are yellow or white. A tennis ball measures about 2.5 inches (6.4 centimeters) across and weighs about 2 ounces (56.7 grams).

Players traditionally wear white, loose-fitting shirts. Loose shirts allow players to swing their arms freely and twist their bodies when hitting the ball. Some modern tennis players wear more colorful clothing.

A pair of good tennis shoes is important. Tennis shoes with rubber soles help prevent slipping when players jump and move for the ball.

Beginners should select an oversized or super-oversized racket head because it has a larger surface area and increased power. As a player improves, he or she can move on to smaller, more maneuverable racket heads.

Tennis rackets come in different sizes and shapes. There are no rules about the racket's weight. The first tennis rackets were made of wood. Modern racket frames are made of lighter materials. These include aluminum, graphite, fiberglass, and titanium. The strings are made with materials such as **gut** and **nylon**. Rubber or leather grips cover the racket handle.

Players sometimes wear wristbands to keep sweat from reaching their hands. It is difficult to hold a tennis racket with sweaty hands.

Male tennis players usually wear gym shorts. Female players can wear shorts or skirts.

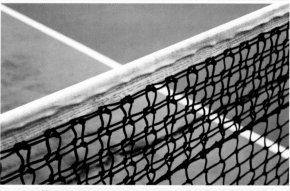

■ In official play, a tennis net must be 3 feet 6 inches (107 centimeters) high at the posts, and 3 feet (91.4 cm) high at the center.

Boundary lines around the tennis court show the play area. The boundary lines are called baselines and **sidelines**. To score a point, the ball must land on or inside the lines.

A service line runs parallel to the baseline. A service centerline runs down the middle of the court from the net to the service line. The service line creates two service boxes. The net runs across the middle of the court, halfway between the baselines.

Tennis courts have three basic surfaces. The most common surface is called hardcourt. A hardcourt surface is made from asphalt or concrete. It is covered with paint mixed with sand to prevent slipping.

Clay courts are made from crushed brick that is packed down and covered by a loose topping of more crushed brick. Some courts are made with very short grass.

■ The sidelines for doubles are wider than the sidelines for singles.

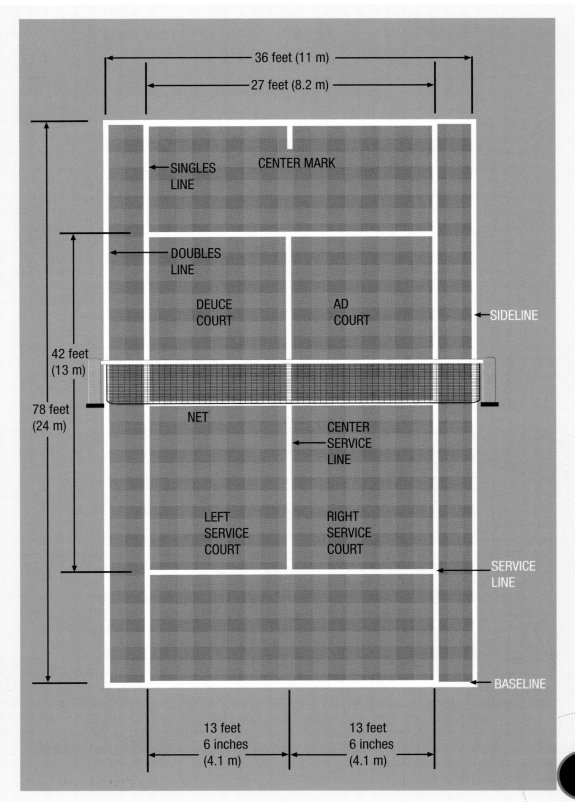

36 feet (11 m)

27 feet (8.2 m)

SINGLES
LINE

CENTER MARK

DOUBLES
LINE

DEUCE
COURT

AD
COURT

SIDELINE

42 feet
(13 m)

NET

CENTER
SERVICE
LINE

78 feet
(24 m)

LEFT
SERVICE
COURT

RIGHT
SERVICE
COURT

SERVICE
LINE

BASELINE

13 feet
6 inches
(4.1 m)

13 feet
6 inches
(4.1 m)

ennis players score points when they hit the ball inside the boundary lines on the opposite side of the court and the **opponent** cannot return it. A player must score four points to win a game, but the player must also have two more points than his or her opponent to win a game. A player wins a set when he or she wins six or more games by two or more games.

A match is made up of games and sets. In **amateur** tennis, the player who wins two out of three sets wins the match. In professional men's tennis, a player must win three out of five sets to win the match. In professional women's tennis, the player who wins two out of three sets wins the match. Matches do not have a time limit. They are won by points alone.

■ Some tennis players use both hands to hit the ball. It gives their swing more power and control.

■ A tiebreaker is played when players are tied at six games. The first player to score seven points and have a lead of two points wins a tiebreaker.

Players decide who **serves** first by tossing a coin or spinning a racket. A player always begins a game by serving beyond the baseline on the right-hand side of the court. The serve alternates between the right and left sides of the court until the game is completed. When the game is completed, the opponent serves the next game.

Tennis players use various shots, or strokes, to keep the ball in play or win points. Groundstrokes are hits made after the ball has bounced once. If the ball bounces twice, it is called dead. The player who serves a ball that becomes dead wins the point. Volleys are hits made before the ball touches the ground. They are exciting to watch.

■ The open stance forehand shot allows players to direct the ball well.

■ One of the most important shots in a player's game is the serve. A strong serve can control the flow of the game.

n both singles and doubles tennis, opponents stand on opposite sides of the court. The player that serves first is called the server. The player on the opposite side and across the court, or cross court, from the server is called the receiver.

The server cannot serve the ball until the receiver is ready. The server has two chances to hit the ball into the service box. If the server misses the service box twice, the receiver wins the point. If the ball hits the net and goes into the service box, the server is given another serve.

■ Serves can be hit with more power and accuracy than any other shot. There are two service boxes on each side of the court. The server aims for the one diagonally across from him or her.

The server cannot step on or over the baseline before serving the ball. This is considered a **fault**. If the serve hits the net or goes out of bounds, it is also a fault.

■ A ball is considered out if it lands outside of the white lines of the court. If the ball touches the line, it is still in play. If a player does not call a ball "out" right away, it is considered "in play."

The receiver can stand anywhere on his or her side of the court. The receiver must let the ball bounce in the service box. If the receiver or a receiver's partner hits the ball before it bounces, the server wins the point.

A player who hits the ball into the net or outside the boundaries of the court loses the point. The ball is still in play if it hits the net and falls onto the opponent's side of the court. A ball that lands on a boundary line is considered in play. A player who does not return a ball that hits the line loses a point.

■ If a ball touches the net for any reason during a serve, it is out of play.

■ Players take turns serving in doubles tennis games.

Playing the Game

Millions of people play tennis around the world. Most of these people are amateurs who play tennis as a recreational sport or in amateur tournaments. The International Tennis Federation (ITF) governs tennis around the world. The ITF oversees 100 national tennis associations.

■ Many colleges and universities have tennis programs in which amateurs can improve their skills. Special training sessions can help children learn the sport.

The organization that oversees competitive amateur tennis in the United States is the United States Tennis Association (USTA). The USTA controls amateur tournaments for children and adults and operates tennis programs for adults. The USTA also offers the U.S. School Tennis program. This program encourages schools to teach students the basics of tennis during physical education classes.

■ Teamwork is very important in doubles tennis. Teams need to work together to cover a wider court.

The Intercollegiate Tennis Association (ITA) oversees college tennis in the United States. The ITA runs a series of four tournaments that ends with the National Collegiate Athletic Association (NCAA) tennis tournament.

Until 1968, professional tennis players were not allowed to play in tournaments. These players earned money playing in **exhibitions**. In 1968, the rules changed, allowing both amateur and professional players to enter tournaments.

Four major tennis tournaments are held each year. The Australian Open is held in Melbourne, Australia. The French Open is held in Paris, France. The Lawn Tennis Championship, or the Wimbledon Championship, is held in London, England. The U.S. Open is held in New York City. These tournaments are called grand slam tournaments.

Players who win one of these tournaments win a Grand Slam title. Winning all four major tournaments, or the Grand Slam, is considered the greatest achievement in tennis.

■ Many children learn how to play tennis between ages four and seven.

Tennis has seen many great players who have inspired today's players.

Arthur Ashe

HOMETOWN: Richmond, Virginia
BIRTHDAY: July 10, 1943

CAREER FACTS:

- Ashe won the 1965 NCAA championship.
- At the 1963 **Davis Cup**, Ashe became the first African American to play on the U.S. team.
- Ashe won three Grand Slam singles titles.
- In 1985, Ashe was inducted to the Tennis Hall of Fame.
- Along with several other players, Ashe founded the Association of Tennis Professionals in 1969.
- Ashe established several charitable organizations, including the National Junior Tennis League, the ABC Cities Tennis Program, the Athlete-Career Connection, and the Safe Passage Foundation.

Björn Borg

HOMETOWN: Sodertalje, Sweden
BIRTHDAY: June 6, 1956

CAREER FACTS:

- In 1973, at 17, Borg was the youngest winner of the Italian Championship.
- Borg was the first Swede to compete in the Davis Cup, in 1975.
- In 1987, Borg was inducted into the International Tennis Hall of Fame.
- Borg won 11 Grand Slam singles titles during his career.
- He won the French Open and Wimbledon in the same year for three consecutive years. Only three players since have been able to win both titles even once. They are Rafael Nadal, Andre Agassi, and Roger Federer.
- Borg retired from tennis at the age of 26.

Steffi Graf

HOMETOWN: Brühl, Germany
BIRTHDAY: June 14, 1969

CAREER FACTS:
- Graf won the Australian Open, French Open, Wimbledon Championship, U.S. Open, and the gold medal at the Summer Olympics in 1988.
  - She was the first person to win the "Golden Grand Slam." This is when a player wins all four Grand Slam tournaments and a gold medal in tennis at the Olympics in one year.
- In 1989, Graf won the Australian Open, Wimbledon Championship, and U.S. Open.
- During her career, Graf won 22 Grand Slam titles.
- Graf won 107 tournaments in her career.
- During her career, Graf was ranked the number one tennis player in the world for 377 weeks.

Pete Sampras

HOMETOWN: Washington, D.C.
BIRTHDAY: August 12, 1971

CAREER FACTS:
- At the age of 19, Sampras became the U.S. Open's youngest male singles champion ever. He beat Andre Agassi in the 1990 final, without losing a set.
- Sampras holds the record for most consecutive year-end World number one titles, with six wins in a row.
- With 14 Grand Slam titles, Sampras held the record for most Grand Slam titles won, until Roger Federer won his 15th in 2009.
- Sampras holds second place in career earnings, with 43 million dollars earned.
- He has won seven Wimbledon singles titles, five U.S. Open singles titles, and two Australian Open titles.

The stars of today are thrilling fans and drawing more people to tennis.

Venus And Serena Williams

VENUS
HOMETOWN: Lynwood, California
BIRTHDAY: June 17, 1980

SERENA
HOMETOWN: Saginaw, Michigan
BIRTHDAY: September 26, 1981

CAREER FACTS:
- Venus won the gold medal at the 2000 Summer Olympics in Sydney, Australia.
- Venus won the Wimbledon Championship and the U.S. Open in 2000 and 2001.
- Serena won the 1999 and 2002 U.S. Open and the 2002 French Open and Wimbledon Championship.
- Serena and Venus were doubles partners at the 2000 Summer Olympics in Sydney, Australia. They won gold medals at the games.
- Together, Venus and Serena have won 26 Grand Slam titles and three Olympic gold medals.

Rafael "Rafa" Nadal Parera

HOMETOWN: Manacor, Mallorca, Spain
BIRTHDAY: June 3, 1986

CAREER FACTS:
- Nadal won the 2008 Olympic gold medal in singles tennis.
- Due to his success playing on clay courts, Nadal has been nicknamed the "The King of Clay."
- Nadal is the first player ever to hold simultaneous Grand Slam titles from games played on clay, grass, and hard court.
- Nadal has won one Australian Open, four French Opens, and one Wimbledon championship.

Andy Roddick

HOMETOWN: Omaha, Nebraska
BIRTHDAY: August 30, 1982

CAREER FACTS:

- Roddick plays best on hard court and grass.
- At the 2004 Davis Cup, Roddick achieved the fastest serve on record at 155 miles per hour (249.5 km/h). He also holds the record for second- and third-fastest serves.
- Roddick also holds the record for the fastest serve in a Grand Slam tournament, at 152 miles per hour (244.6 km/h).
- With 39 wins at Wimbledon 2009, Roddick holds the record for most games won in a Grand Slam.

Roger Federer

HOMETOWN: Basel, Switzerland
BIRTHDAY: August 8, 1981

CAREER FACTS:

- Many sports analysts, tennis specialists, and tennis players believe Federer is the best tennis player ever.
- From February 2, 2004, until August 17, 2008, Federer was ranked number one, giving him a men's record 237 consecutive weeks at the top.
- With 15 Grand Slam singles titles, Federer holds the record for most Grand Slams won.
- Federer has appeared in more Grand Slam finals than any other player.
- Federer has won three Australian Opens, one French Open, six Wimbledon championships, and five U.S. Opens.

Exercise, such as tennis, keeps people fit and healthy. Eating a balanced diet helps, too. Eating fruits and vegetables provides necessary vitamins. Breads, pasta, and rice are sources of food energy. Meats supply protein for building muscles. Dairy products have calcium, which builds strong bones. Eating foods from all the food groups every day keeps a tennis player's body in top condition.

Drinking plenty of water before, during, and after tennis is important. Water helps keep people's bodies cool. Tennis players should avoid sugary drinks. Sugary drinks do not **hydrate** the body as quickly as water.

■ Tennis players lose water through sweat. Drinking water replaces what has been lost.

■ Eating salad is a good way to add a variety of fruits and vegetables to an athlete's diet.

Strong, flexible muscles are important for playing tennis. Training the right muscles a few times every week makes playing tennis more fun and prevents injuries. Stretching keeps muscles flexible. It is best to stretch during and after a **warmup**. Warmup exercises include running in place for a few minutes and running laps.

Tennis players need strong legs for quick movements. Jumping in place makes legs strong. When jumping in place, many tennis players lift their knees as high as possible on each jump. Players also need strong hands and fingers. To work these muscles, squeeze a tennis ball in each hand several times.

■ Sometimes, tennis players develop a sore and tender elbow. Gentle stretching exercises help prevent this type of injury.

Test your knowledge of this great sport by trying to answer these tennis brain teasers!

1 What shape was the first tennis court?

2 Where was lawn tennis first played?

3 If a serve hits the net or goes out of bounds, what is it called?

4 What are the names of the four Grand Slam tournaments?

5 What is the time limit for tennis games?

6 What substances are most tennis courts made of?

Glossary

amateur: a person who is not paid to play a game and who may not have much experience

baselines: the back boundary lines at each end of a tennis court

competitors: people who play against each other in sports events

Davis Cup: the biggest international men's tennis team competition in the world; played each year

exhibitions: public performances

fault: a serve that breaks the rules

gut: a strong cord made from the intestines of sheep

hydrate: to provide water to maintain a proper balance of fluids

inflated: filled with air

nylon: a strong fabric made from chemicals

opponent: a player that is against another in a game

serves: puts the ball in play by hitting it

sidelines: lines that mark the side boundaries of a tennis court

spectator: a person who watches a game but does not play

synthetic: man-made or artificial

tournament: competition in which contestants play a series of games to decide the winner

warmup: gentle exercise to prepare a person's body for stretching and game play

Index

Ashe, Arthur 16
Australian Open 15, 17, 18, 19, 22

ball 5, 6, 8, 10, 11, 12, 13, 21
baselines 5, 8, 9, 11, 12
Borg, Bjorn 16

court 5, 8, 9, 10, 11, 12, 13, 14, 18, 19, 22

Davis Cup 16, 19
doubles 5, 8, 9, 12, 13, 14, 18

Federer, Roger 16, 17, 19
French Open 15, 16, 17, 18, 19, 22

Graf, Steffi 17

net 5, 7, 8, 9, 12, 13, 22

Olympics 17, 18

Parera, Rafael Nadal 18

racket 5, 6, 7, 11
Roddick, Andy 19

Sampras, Pete 17
score 8, 10
shoes 6
sidelines 8, 9
singles 5, 8, 9, 12, 16, 17, 18, 19

tournament 5, 14, 15, 17, 19, 22

U.S. Open 15, 17, 18, 19, 22

Williams, Serena 18
Williams, Venus 18
Wimbledon Championship 5, 15, 16, 17, 18, 19, 22
Wingfield, Major Walter C. 5

Log on to www.av2books.com

AV² by Weigl brings you media enhanced books that support active learning. Go to **www.av2books.com**, and enter the special code inside the front cover of this book. You will gain access to enriched and enhanced content that supplements and complements this book. Content includes video, audio, web links, quizzes, a slide show, and activities.

Audio
Listen to sections of the book read aloud.

Video
Watch informative video clips.

Web Link
Find research sites and play interactive games.

Try This!
Complete activities and hands-on experiments.

WHAT'S ONLINE?

 **Try This!** Complete activities and hands-on experiments.	**Web Link** Find research sites and play interactive games.	**Video** Watch informative video clips.	**EXTRA FEATURES**
Pages 6-7 Test your knowledge of tennis equipment.	**Pages 4-5** Find out more information about the history of tennis.	**Pages 4-5** View a video about tennis.	**Audio** Hear introductory audio at the top of every page
Pages 8-9 Use this activity to test how well you know the tennis court.	**Pages 8-9** Learn more about the tennis court.	**Pages 18-19** View an interview with one of the world's top tennis players.	**Key Words** Study vocabulary, and play a matching word game.
Pages 12-13 See how well you know the rules of tennis.	**Pages 10-11** Learn more about keeping score in tennis.		**Slide Show** View images and captions, and try a writing activity.
Pages 16-17 Write a biography about one of the superstars of tennis.	**Pages 12-13** Read about tennis rules and regulations.		**AV² Quiz** Take this quiz to test your knowledge
Pages 20-21 Play an interactive game.	**Pages 14-15** Learn about playing tennis.		
Page 22 Test your tennis knowledge.	**Pages 20-21** Find out more about eating healthy foods.		